Lectionary Poems, Year A

For Cynthia,

    — disciple of the man for
               others,

    — faithful servant of the
             church,

    — good friend.

          Scott

          2/7/20

Lectionary Poems, Year A

Surprising Grace for Pulpit and Pew

*Poems for each Sunday and other special days
of the church year based on texts from the
Revised Common Lectionary, Year A*

SCOTT L. BARTON

RESOURCE *Publications* • Eugene, Oregon

LECTIONARY POEMS, YEAR A
Surprising Grace for Pulpit and Pew

Resource Publications
An Imprint of Wipf and Stock Publishers
199 W. 8th Ave., Suite 3
Eugene, OR 97401

www.wipfandstock.com

PAPERBACK ISBN: 978-1-7252-5306-3
HARDCOVER ISBN: 978-1-7252-5307-0
EBOOK ISBN: 978-1-7252-5308-7

Manufactured in the U.S.A.   04/18/19

Dedicated to Elizabeth H. Sarfaty,
who, like the importunate widow,
kept after me until she, and you,
finally got this book;

and to Paul "Pappy" Heller,
who, along with Darlene,
is a mark of the faithfulness of God;

and to Gayle,
whose encouragement of
such ministerial pursuits as this
is heavenly.

May the God of hope fill you with all joy and peace in believing, so that you may abound in hope by the power of the Holy Spirit.

Romans 15:13

Contents

Introduction

While I was sitting in the pew in worship recently, a man walked to the pulpit from among the congregation to give the scripture reading for the day. The bulletin told me that the text was from the Revelation to John. I was eagerly anticipating some surprising news to which the preacher would later give context. But, first, it was the power of the written word that I was anticipating being boldly proclaimed.

Instead, the reader got to the pulpit, looked at the congregation, and said jovially, "Good morning!" Of course, that was the congregation's cue to say "Good morning!" back. And, with that exchange, the wind was knocked out of the sails of the reading to come. Before any other words came out of the reader's mouth, the text was domesticated and made, in my opinion, palatable, predictable, and pedestrian. We were told, in two words, neither to expect the unexpected nor to be blown away.

Forty years ago, Annie Dillard wrote in *Teaching A Stone to Talk* that we should all wear crash helmets to church, which I took to mean that we always ought to expect the unexpected when it comes to encounters with God. The main place Protestants, at least historically, expected to encounter God was in the written word. Roman Catholics have rediscovered the same. But, Christians of all stripes are always in danger of thinking that, since we have heard a text before, we know what it says. "Ho, hum, the reading of Scripture," the old critique went. So, in both our public and private readings, it can feel as if we are just going through the motions in order to reinforce what we already know. But, as Martin Luther wrote in *Preface of the Old Testament*, "[T]hink of the Scriptures as the loftiest and noblest of holy things, as the richest of mines, which can never be exhausted . . . " (*The Complete Works of Dr. Martin Luther*, St. Louis German Edition,

XIV, 3–4). There is always more than meets the eye, or maybe I should say, than we think we see. So, our job is to look, and to expect to have our socks knocked off.

With these poems, I am trying to help you see that the biblical text can still knock your socks off. In their own ways, both liberal and fundamentalist Christianity have made us forget this essential quality of scripture. By intellectually explaining, or moralistically opining, much of our Christian culture is missing the mined richness of the written word. Like the last line or two of many a poem, I am convinced that the text provides "zingers" that have the capacity to make us laugh, smile, cry "Wow!" and sit up and take notice of a grace that breaks through in ways that the writers and earliest faith communities found amazing and bold. I hope these poems will help you notice things you never did before in the lectionary readings. I am also hoping they provide you with a way of thinking about the weekly sermon—preparing it, and listening to it.

Like the various ways of appreciating any text, the poems themselves have a variety of rhyme and meter. Sometimes the meter is determined by something straight from the text that "grabbed" me so much I just needed to lead with it. Sometimes it is a simple iambic pentameter. Sometimes the poem is in a rhyming, Dr. Seuss-like anapestic tetrameter, for who better brought out a child-like joy with words (and here we're dealing with *the* word)? Sometimes the free verse should just freely let the Spirit lead you.

The important thing in all these poems, which are in their own way mini-sermons, is to read the biblical text or texts first, and then keep the page open. Keep an open mind about it. Do not presuppose any so-called meaning. Put aside any doctrine you once learned that is "supported" by a text. Let the main doctrine always be the surprising grace shown in both Original and New Testaments that almost begs you not to miss it because it is told in so many ways. Finally, read the poems, and even the biblical texts, out loud first. Remember, the texts are all proclamations! So, proclaim, if only to yourself!

Now, have fun! May the text and these poems speak with joy to both your mind and heart.

Scott L. Barton
Pelham, Massachusetts

THE FIRST SUNDAY OF ADVENT (A)—
ISAIAH 2:1–5; MATTHEW 24:36–44

Two poems for preachers, although in the second poem, "Christian" could be substituted for "preacher."

Isaiah 2:1–5

No Sermon Necessary?

Oh, how can you improve upon this poem?
Isaiah is the master of the verse.
To read this text, delib'rately and bold,
The one up front who's preaching could do worse
Than simply look out on the people there
With hope that some day, all of us might hear
The One who calls all people as God's own,
All tribes and factions, with our pride and fear.
The reason that someday we'll beat those swords
Into the implements that would us feed,
Is that we'll know the love God has for all,
Including those of different breeds and creeds.
Reflecting on this hope and faith and dream,
O, preacher, end the reading with a grin;
Then close the book, look out at those you love,
And in the silence, let it all sink in.

Matthew 24:36–44

Freed for Love

Oh, woe to the preacher who parses this text
To figure out how and when Jesus comes next;
For those of the "left behind" ilk are the folk
Who build their theology on such a joke
As worrying whether they all might be saved!
But Jesus calls "worry" a trip to the grave!
For back in verse three, when his friends sought to know
The timetable for the world's powers' overthrow,
He gave this long discourse so they all might see,
The one thing in life that's God's sure guarantee:
Today is your chance to see Christ in your deeds;
Leave end times to God—so for love you'll be freed!

THE SECOND SUNDAY OF ADVENT (A)—
ISAIAH 11:1–10; MATTHEW 3:1–12

Isaiah 11:1–10

Time to Remember

A shoot shall come from Jesse's stump,
A branch from his roots sure will grow,
God's spirit of wisdom,
And right understanding,
The fear of the LORD shall he know.

The wolf shall then live with the lamb,
The leopard shall lie with the kid,
The calf and the lion,
The fatling together,
Shall all by a child be led.

These words from Isaiah all point
To one who would someday be born,
Whom we know and expect
With our houses bedecked,
When waiting will end Christmas morn.

And now is the time to recall
He favors the poor and the meek;
So that none be destroyed,
He our walls would avoid,
Let us Christ, show and tell, breathe and speak.

Matthew 3:1–12

Full Communion

He's not very Christmassy,
this John the B.,
to people presuming that
they're guaranteed
to have the good life because
priv'leged they are;
But when the one born, who was
brought gifts of myrrh,
reveals a new twist on what
John thought would come,
the world can now know that all
judging succumbs
to he who now chooses to
make from the grain
the bread of his life, so we'll
drink in love's reign.

THE THIRD SUNDAY OF ADVENT (A)—
ISAIAH 35:1–10; MATTHEW 11:2–11

Isaiah 35:1–10

After Disaster

Apparently, you can go home again.
At least, Isaiah has the nerve to think
You can return to what you knew deep down,
Although you drank disaster's bitter drink.

Perhaps it's when you rediscover how,
You were assured, as children, all was right;
Perhaps it's when old innocence you find,
And speaking truth, assume they'll see the light.

Although the pain of what was past remains,
Still, strengthen hands; make firm the feeble knees;
Proclaim to those who love, "Be strong! Fear not!"
God will restore us from such times as these.

Matthew 11:2–11

A Messiah Like That

To a contractor I have said,
"Are you the one who is to come,
Or shall we wait for another?"
Now let's say I ask it this week,
Since now my particular need
Is getting a load of firewood;
But what if the answer I hear is,
"I am heating peoples' houses
For their entire lives, not just
One load at a time. Pretty cool!"
Would I risk it? Would I believe?
Or would my faith be just in what
I can see—my wood, the stove's flame?
The Preposterous One does more
Than you or I can imagine:
People see the light! Get moving!!
They're no longer outcast!!! They hear!!!!
Their spirits are no longer dead!!!!!
AND THE POOR EVEN HAVE GOOD NEWS!!!!!!
(Can you tell Matthew's shouting now?)

A Messiah like that may be
A better bargain than you thought.

THE FOURTH SUNDAY OF ADVENT (A)—
ISAIAH 7:10-16; MATTHEW 1:18-25

Isaiah 7:10-16

The Girl with the Virgin Brand

Who is this girl of whom Isaiah speaks,
Who, soon, would bear a child, and thus critique
The lack of faith that Ahaz came to bear
Upon the country that was in his care?
The child's name, Immanuel, would show
God's people then (and now!) they'd ne'er outgrow
Their need to trust that God was in their midst.
This pedigree of faith, which wasn't missed
By Matthew or by Luke, would then describe
A mother and her child, who would inscribe
Upon the hearts of people for all time
A birth we celebrate, and call sublime.

Matthew 1:18–25

What's in a Name?

What's in a name? Look at them here!
Jesus—the Messiah—Mary—
Joseph—Holy Spirit—the Lord—
David—Emmanuel—Jesus—
And the main character gets three!
This introduction, this prologue,
This tale to whet the appetite,
Foreshadows many other names:
Door—good shepherd—way—truth—life—bread—
Lamb of God—Rabbi—Son of God—
King of Israel—Savior—Lord;
Perhaps the baby reminds us
That he by any other name
Would smell as sweet.

CHRISTMAS EVE/THE NATIVITY OF JESUS CHRIST—LUKE 2:1–20

When History Repeats Itself

It was a terrifying time
Which we, by faith, now think sublime;
But then, a madman on the throne
Drove everyone away from home,
That everyone be taxed and counted;
But this, in point of fact, amounted
To terrorism by the high
Who gave no choice but to comply.

Think, immigrants; think, refugees;
Think how all those of low degree
In every age are made to do
The bidding of a mighty few.
Think those who fear they'll be deported,
Their work, and fam'ly life now thwarted;
Think those from bombed-out cities fleeing,
What kind of news would bring well-being?

Imagine they see in the flesh,
Perhaps in angels and a crèche,
Or maybe, solidarity
With those who bear Christ's guarantee
That he'll be with us all our days!
Then they, as well, might be amazed—
Like shepherds hearing angel choirs—
What real love from God requires.

Thus into angst and grief and fears
The God of every soul appears,
Yes, then, but also here, today,
And bids us live just as we pray.

To Make Our Love Braver

She did something different,
She treasured and pondered;
Not only amazed, but
She thought, and she wondered
Just what was their meaning—
That this diapered wee boy,
Would be to all people
The sign of a great joy?

And why even now does
He cause such a flutter
In hearts all around, while
These carols we utter?
Is this what they meant when
They said that a savior
Would come—a Messiah,
To make our love braver?

Solstice

"It's the big night!"
Is what my father used to say,
And then in June,
It was, "Tomorrow's the big day!"
—Thus, the solstice
Always arrives for me with mirth,
Which may be what
We need to hear about this birth
Announced each year!
The angel told with twinkling eyes
—Thus, cast out fear—
So they would laugh with great surprise;
Despite the dark,
This same news called to you this night
Begs to be told,
That Love may be our solstice light.

They Thought It Was the Feds

Perhaps they thought it was the Feds who'd come for them!
Somehow, the N.S.A. had tracked, and would condemn
Those dirty shepherds, since they had not registered,
And since, without green cards, Augustus' wrath incurred!
But soon they found the searchlight not to be the law,
Which, with relief, provoked a different kind of awe;
That is, more powerful than all the "powers that be,"
Was then announced—as now—the holy mystery:
Quite openly, the one who saves comes not by strength
Of arm, but will not fail to go to any length
For love! Thus wrapped, so even shepherds might embrace
This child, we, too, now hold our breath, to see such grace.

(originally published in *The Presbyterian Outlook*, December 9, 2013)

THE FIRST SUNDAY AFTER CHRISTMAS DAY (A)— ISAIAH 63:7–9; MATTHEW 2:13–23

Isaiah 63:7–9

Not Just in Days of Old

God knows it's not enough to talk,
So God comes by to visit,
To lift, to carry those God loves
E'en when they fail to "get it."
The point of God has always been
That grace, you cannot lose it;
To those who fear, love sidles near,
So anxious folk might cool it.

Matthew 2:13–23

The Two Josephs

It seems to me I've heard this song before;
Remember Joseph, by his dad, adored,
Who, off to Egypt went one day, enslaved,
As good as dead, his brothers so depraved
They'd even murder just to guarantee
He'd bloom no more upon the fam'ly tree?

But then, in dreams, we see that God persists
In showing that God all the while insists
That even though a tyrant's on the throne,
Those loved by God will never stand alone.

Again weeps Rachel—God abandons not—
And this new dreaming Joseph finds a spot
To raise the child born with no silver spoon!
—All to the end that we might be attuned
To hear the old familiar score, known well;
And yearning, searching love for all, retell.

THE EPIPHANY OF THE LORD—ISAIAH 60:1-6
AND MATTHEW 2:1-12; ALSO MICAH 5:2-5a

Off by Nine Miles

You have to be careful in choosing a text
When trying to figure what God will do next;
The wise men, it seems, had Isaiah in mind,
For in chapter 60, the prophet assigned
Jerusalem as the location for light
To shine, with the glory of Yahweh so bright
The wealth of the nations around it would come!
With frankincense, camels, and gold they'd become
Disciples! From darkness, God's glory'd redound
To those who'd kept faith, and would now be renowned!

But wise can be wrong—they were off by nine miles!
The text that they needed was just not God's style,
For Micah had said that a town, oh so small,
Would bring forth the one to be shepherd of all!
Poor Herod (the rich) also knew not this text,
And sent for the scribes of the people, perplexed
Because of the ruler his visitors sought;
Not wise, nor the powerful, ever had thought
A prophet from out in the country could know
A place such as Bethlehem ever could show
The world a new ruler who'd ever increase
The good of the world with his treasure of peace.

(Based on Walter Brueggemann's imagining, in *The Christian Century* [December 19, 2001] and in *Inscribing the Text* [Fortress, 2004], that the wise men were off by nine miles after picking the wrong text.)

THE BAPTISM OF THE LORD (A)—
ISAIAH 42:1–9 AND MATTHEW 3:13–17

Why Does It Matter that Jesus Was Baptized?

Why does it matter that Jesus was baptized?
Only that you really join him right there—
Into the water you go, as John holds you,
Then there's the voice as you gasp in fresh air;
Yes, of the Maker of all, you're beloved!
Chosen, and in whom our God is well-pleased;
How do I know this? Isaiah says, clearly,
"Servant" means people whom God dearly sees
As those who are called to bring justice to all;
God is delighted with such a great scheme!
Taking God's people in hand as we step out,
We are God's servants, whose work's to redeem
People from darkness, injustice, and prison;
We will not whine, nor our spirits be quenched—
Jesus was baptized, so we, as God's people,
With water and spirit our lives might be drenched!

THE SECOND SUNDAY IN ORDINARY TIME/
SECOND AFTER THE EPIPHANY (A)—
ISAIAH 49:1–7; JOHN 1:29–42

Isaiah 49:1–17

Proof Text

This text is proof you cannot separate
First person singular from plural—
At least not when it comes to faith,
Where one's salvation is no cure-all;
Isaiah segues back and forth,
The "me" once named and called, the nation,
But noting that he's called, as well,
Proclaims both born God's good creation.
The nation and the prophet, both,
Were called by God to be a blessing,
Through thick and thin, though down and out,
Our job's God's love for all professing.

John 1:29–42

What's in a Name (Again)?

This is another text brimming with names,
"Here is the Lamb of God," the Baptist claims;
Then it's not long until "Lamb" is "the Son!"
Thinking of these, I then wonder, "Which one?"
Lamb of God? Son of God? Which will it be?
Maybe there is a progression to see?
But, two disciples of John start with this—
"Rabbi!" they say (although not with a kiss!)
Then it's not long 'til "Messiah" he's called!
Don't get attached to one name above all,
John (the Evangelist) here seems to say;
Jesus is more than just one sobriquet—
Son of God, Rabbi, Messiah, or Lamb,
Jesus is surely, "I am who I am!"
You and I, too, aren't just stuck in one place,
"Simon" can quickly be "Cephas," by grace;
Maybe it just all depends where you are—
What you are called—when, what matters, by far:
You are inscribed on the walls of God's heart,
Brimming with love, which for you, won't depart.

THE THIRD SUNDAY IN ORDINARY TIME/THIRD AFTER THE EPIPHANY (A)—ISAIAH 9:1-4; MATTHEW 4:12-23

Isaiah 9:1-4

Inaugurating Hope

When gloom spreads wide upon the land,
And darkness from a firebrand
Spews forth in ways unthinkable,
Each speech and tweeted syllable
Anathema to who you are,
Hear this: No help comes from afar,
But from the news no news feed brings,
Which peasants, workers, queens, and kings
Alike have known from age to age:
The Lord of light will e'er upstage
Pretenders to the throne of grace,
So all might see, and all embrace
A world where light for all might shine,
And where God's people still align
Themselves with those called "least of these,"
Thus multiplying love that frees.

Matthew 4:12–23

Waste Not, Want Not

Two brothers picked, and then, two more,
And when those pairs both come ashore
It's almost like, in these first calls,
He wastes not, wants not, by this haul,
Where with economy of words,
He's quickly gathered up one third
The crew! Who knew he's in a rush?
But with conviction, now, he's flush,
For when he sees John's likely fate,
It's time to fish, not just cut bait!
He doesn't stop to analyze—
Or these guys' qualities apprise—
He simply calls; they simply go;
And not just there, or long ago,
But even now he calls all kinds:
His love is now for hearts and minds.

THE FOURTH SUNDAY IN ORDINARY TIME/
FOURTH AFTER THE EPIPHANY (A)—
MICAH 6:1–8; MATTHEW 5:1–12 AND
1 CORINTHIANS 1:18–31

Micah 6:1–8

The Controversy of the LORD

"The controversy of the LORD"
Is written by the prophet to restore
The right relationship between
A people who believe, and God not seen.

He argues, he contends; his "rib"*
(In Hebrew) means much more than he's just peeved,
Or that his nose is out of joint;
He brings a lawsuit now to make a point.

That point is this: There is no God
That you can claim unless you think it's odd
That you have gotten where you are
Apart from being such a shining star.

The word, my friends, says Micah, still,
Is gratitude that is unproved until
The kindness, love and justice shown
To you, from you to others will be known.

* רִיב complaint, suit, contention

Matthew 5:1–12 and 1 Corinthians 1:18–31

Blessed Are the Upside Down

"Blessed are the upside down,"
So he seems to say; But—
Who on earth is glad to mourn?
What blessing is conveyed?
Likewise, poor in spirit—Who
Is happy to be there?
Meek folks aren't on *Forbes*'s list,
Such combination's rare;
No good deed goes unpunished,
The cynic wryly notes;
But kingdom view is different!
—And henceforth, faith denotes
Not wisdom for a sampler,
To hang upon the wall,
But vision upside down is—
God's vision, above all!
The good news is God sees things
To which we're mostly blind,
Unless we look with Jesus,
His heart, and soul and mind;
Things that are not, will yet be,
And God counts no one out;
Each one belongs to God, and,
Thus, blessed are you!—No doubt!

(The opening line is from a sermon by Barbara Brown Taylor, in *Gospel Medicine*, [Rowman & Littlefield, 1995].)

THE FIFTH SUNDAY IN ORDINARY TIME/FIFTH AFTER THE EPIPHANY (A)— ISAIAH 58:1-9a (9b-12); MATTHEW 5:13-20;

Isaiah 58:1–9a (9b–12)

Here I Am!

Have you ever noticed, "Here I am,"
That great response to the great "I am?"
So many say it throughout the text,
But then, Easy Street is never next!
Abraham says it first to the LORD,
And then, to Isaac, while holding a sword;
And then a third time back to his God,
Each time portends a challenge so odd
You worry for the one who spoke it,
Since what those words all seem to transmit
Is something so scary up ahead
It's like a cue, filling you with dread.
For Esau, Jacob, and Joseph, too;
And then again, when Israel, who
Heard words that he should be not afraid,
Feared, by sons, he'd again be betrayed!
Moses says it to that burning bush,
Then, Samuel, when, from sleeping, is pushed
To go to old Eli, speaks times five
These words; which means he could be deprived
Of life and limb, since answ'ring that call
Some day means he'll stand up to Saul!
The Psalmist, too, then risks offending
Those who would mock his faith unending;
And finally, Jeremiah risks it;
We hold our breaths, 'til he's acquitted.

But guess what? The LORD says such words, too!
In Isaiah, these same words construe
The risk God takes not to be swayed by
Our words, unless it's love we live by.

So when it comes
to love, I guess,
There's no such thing
as no duress.

(The references to "Here I Am!" above are to Gen. 22:1, 7, 11; 27:1, 18; 31:11; 37:13; 46:2; Exod. 3:4; 1 Sam. 3:4, 5, 6, 8, 16; Ps. 40:7; Jer. 26:14; and Isa. 65:1, as well as our text, Isa. 58:9.)

Matthew 5:13–20

Alternate Fact

Jesus used an alternate fact
Because they knew: Salt cannot lack
For taste, no matter what they say;
Nor can a city on a hill
Be hid, no matter what you will;
Boxed up, a new lamp doesn't stay,
But everyone will plug it in
For light—there is no other spin;
Such facts stood then, and stand today.

And you are like that lamp and salt,
Existing so you might exalt
The one whose love has made you so;
This fact no one can take away,
And thus, the rules of love will stay!
God's people from them shall not go,
And need each day to demonstrate
That neighbor-caring cannot wait,
In towns and cities, high or low.

THE SIXTH SUNDAY IN ORDINARY TIME/
SIXTH AFTER THE EPIPHANY (A)—
DEUTERONOMY 30:15–20; MATTHEW 5:21–37

Deuteronomy 30:15–20

The River We Crossed

Perhaps by now we're too removed
From when our ancestors improved
Their lives by coming to this land,
Since far too many now command
A blanket prohibition to
The people who don't look like you
Against their coming 'cross the sea—
Forgetting that the guarantee
Of blessings is to keep in mind
God's people e'er have been defined
By their rememb'ring whence they came,
And still by love, God's love proclaim.

Matthew 5:21–37

Like a Poem

Is this just an ideal time
He posits, where reason and rhyme
Will fin'lly rule the way we live?
Or do his words an image give
Of faith right now, where anger, lust,
And all the things that he discussed
—Which cause us woe—make us averse
To let our lives by them be cursed?
This "You have heard it said, but I . . ."
Reveals that he's the reason why
We, too, might live with trust and thanks,
And—surprise!— on unmetered love now bank.

THE SEVENTH SUNDAY IN ORDINARY TIME/ SEVENTH AFTER THE EPIPHANY (A)—LEVITICUS 19:1-2, 9-18; MATTHEW 5:38-48 (SEE ALSO LEVITICUS 24:20)

Leviticus 19:1-2, 9-18

Come Again?

Oh, how so many seem to think
That Jesus taught an innovation,
That love for others as yourself
Was born after his incarnation;
But he, a Jew, knew well his faith,
And said anew just what the text does;
He simply spoke with grace and joy,
And put his money where his mouth was.

Matthew 5:38–48 (see also Leviticus 24:20)

Christian Evolution

Consider *lex talionis*,
That wonderful innovation
The Jews invented for us all.
It had been a life for an eye,
A clan for a life, and a tribe
For a clan—justice meant revenge;
But eye for eye was radical;
Life for life was retributive,
Not revenge, not "We are god now."
Give thanks for Leviticus, then;
Give thanks for that step that allowed
Jesus to go one step further.
It's the progression of faith, see?
I guess evolution always
Takes a very long time to get
To where God wants us all to be.

*Bonus Poem for the kids for this Sunday,
based on the Matthew text*

An eye for an eye, a tooth for a tooth,
Makes the whole world blind,
A better weapon you can use
Is always keep in mind
That you are still a child of God
No matter what your pain,
And so's the other person, too,
Although I can't explain
Just why that's true! But God loves more
Than you or I can guess,
And when we all can learn that fact,
Is when we'll all be blest.

TRANSFIGURATION SUNDAY— MATTHEW 17:1-9 (10-21). A HYMN FOR WORSHIP

Crucified Lord Who Rose So We Might Live

(NICAEA)

Scott L. Barton (2014) John Bacchus Dykes (1861)

Holy, holy, holy! Lord God Almighty!
After six days, you took them up the mountainside,
There a new defining, in your face all shining,
You, our new Moses, ever here abide.

We have come before you, seeking to adore you,
In this sanctuary, our songs to you we raise,
Your word still astounds us, grace for all surrounds us,
Our love for you, and all, our greatest praise.

There is no delaying, for we hear you saying,
"Follow where I go, and cure the sick and heal the lame;
Folk of every label, welcome to my table,
Fear not, by faith, my love to all proclaim."

Holy, holy, holy! Lord God Almighty!
Now we go returning, out to the world you give;
Traveling together, through all kinds of weather,
Crucified Lord, who rose so we might live!

ASH WEDNESDAY (A)—ISAIAH 58:1-12

Ticket to Ride

Remember you are dust,
To dust you shall return,
We're all terminal on this bus,
But maybe we can learn
Today, because that's true,
To look outside ourselves,
So, when we leave our pews,
By love we're now compelled
To choose the kind of fast
That makes the oppressed go free,
That welcomes the harassed,
And those of low degree.
May we repair the breach,
The streets to live, restore,
And by our acts so preach
That hate will be no more.

("We are all terminal on this bus" is from Anne Lamott's *Bird by Bird* [Anchor, 1995].)

THE FIRST SUNDAY IN LENT (A)—
GENESIS 2:15-17, 3:1-7; MATTHEW 4:1-11

Genesis 2:15-17, 3:1-7

What's Really Original Here

The LORD God governs by the seat of his pants
In this passage, or so it seems.
He creates the man, and then
Has the idea to put him in the garden.

Why didn't he create him in the garden in the first place, and save a step?

He commands the man that he may eat of every tree.
Oh, wait, he thinks. Maybe not.
Scratch that idea of eating from the tree
Of the knowledge of good and evil.

So why did he start out with "every," anyway, so he had to backtrack?

God comes up with the brilliant punishment
Of death, not just someday, but on that day,
The day when the man might eat from the tree
That's now forbidden.

What kind of God issues idle threats, anyway, unless he's just making it up?

The text doesn't absolve God from responsibility, either:
He's the one who made a crafty wild animal.
Plus (before the invention of Dr. Doolittle),
One who talks! And is understood!

Why create a talking, crafty animal in the first place?

Apparently, God is protective of his place in the scheme of things.
At least (if the serpent knows the score)
God would prefer the man not be like him,
Which means, knowing good and evil.

Okay, the obvious, now: So why make that tree in the first place?

Now, before she has the knowledge of good and evil,
The woman sees that the fruit is good for food
And was a delight to the eyes
And was to be desired to make one wise.

Does she have any say in the matter? Whence delight? And who is the
subject of that last passive phrase—unless it's God?

Apparently, the man, not quite as quick-witted, didn't see the things
the woman did.
He was with her, but maybe he was wondering
How all of a sudden he got to be this woman's husband,
Without benefit of clergy, and all.

And how could he be a husband (and she a wife?) if they didn't know
a good thing when they saw it yet?

They eat the fruit, and their eyes are opened.
And all of a sudden they get the concept of nakedness!
And sewing! And metaphor!
(I mean, presumably, nobody had woven loincloth yet!)

There are way too many questions here.

Why do we have to do backflips to make sense of this tale?
Why spoil it with something nowhere to be found in the text?
Why not call it original *relationship*? Because, really.
Isn't that what this new, astonishing God wants with you and me, a
little give and take?

A little, well . . . love?

Matthew 4:1–11

When the Spirit Drove Jesus to Have His Retreat

When the Spirit drove Jesus to have his retreat,
It was hardly a route that you'd call Easy Street,
For the things that he saw when he got there were spare,
Such as no food in sight for a forty-day prayer!
Then Old Satan arrived with a tempting repast:
"Turn these stones into bread—or have you been miscast?"
Deuteronomy, then, was what Jesus recalled,
When the writer tells Israel their daily haul
Of the manna was given so they'd always know
(And not only in places and times long ago)
That it's not just by bread that we find we're restored,
But by every word from the mouth of the Lord;
Next, the devil took Jesus way up to the top
Of the temple, where there, it's as if they talked shop!
Yes, the devil quotes scripture, in this case, a Psalm,
To which Jesus responds, with a certain aplomb,
—Deuteronomy still on his mind—that a test
Of the Lord surely misses the point that we're blessed
By the places we've been with the Lord as our guide,
Giving all that we need, since by love, God provides!
Then the tempter took Jesus to see from up high
All the kingdoms below, and then added his lie
About having it all, if for him, he'd declare;
But again, Deuteronomy calls us to swear
Our allegiance to God, and the Lord only serve,
Since for freedom, by grace, have our lives been preserved;
Now the devil was bested, and angels arrived
And they waited on he whom our spirits revive;
Thus we see here in Jesus the road that he took,
Which he did on his own, but he did by the book.

(Written with Theodore Geisel (Dr. Seuss) in mind, born March 2, 1904, who often wrote
in rhyming anapestic tetrameter. Think Yertle the Turtle, tempted to get way up high!)

THE SECOND SUNDAY IN LENT (A)— PSALM 121; JOHN 3:1–17 (SEE ALSO JOHN 7:45–53 AND 19:38–42); JOHN 3:1–17 (SEE ALSO NUMBERS 21:9)

Psalm 121

The Funeral

How many know these words by heart,
With memory of open graves,
And lives, so rudely torn apart,
All looking for some word to save,

Not make it better, or remove
The grief and tears by something said,
Nor some far afterlife to prove
By news of rising from the dead,

But a connection make to those
Who also looked for help above,
And finding mountains lacking, chose
To trust that all was made in love;

For only love can heal the heart,
Can keep you well, can be your shade,
Can keep you, e'en when you depart—
Is even why you dared to pray.

John 3:1–17 (see also John 7:45–53 and 19:38–42)

Winded

Nicodemus knew
That Jesus was on to something
With all that talk
About being born from above,
Even though he hadn't a clue
Of the wind's comings and goings.
Thus he went to that meeting
Where the blowhards
Wanted to do Jesus in,
And tried to talk some sense into them.
I wonder where he got such courage,
Going again by night,
The weight of the world on his back,
Or at least a hundred pounds,
To bury his rabbi,
Winded by the law of love?

John 3:1–17 (see also Numbers 21:9)

Divine

It's not just at a football game
Where you will see the sign
That God so loved the world, God gave
God's son; for now "divine"
Means whatsoe'er is given from
The bottom of the heart;
And when that comes, like wind, unplanned,
You'll find your life can start
Again! You're born as if anew,
Since you've looked up to see
The love which from all poison now
Has set the whole world free.

THE THIRD SUNDAY IN LENT (A)—
EXODUS 17:1-7 AND JOHN 4:5-42; ROMANS 5:1-11

Exodus 17:1-7 and John 4:5-42

Three Drinking Limericks

"Is the LORD now among us, or not?"
Cried the thirsty and quarreling tribe;
Thus when Moses told God,
The response, "Use the rod!"
Meant by striking the rock, they imbibed.

"Woman, give me some water to drink,"
Jesus, to the Samaritan said,
But if drink he received,
We can't tell, or perceive—
What we learn is, she drank in, instead.

Thus we hear that refreshment is giv'n,
When for water or love we might thirst,
When we think it's our job
To prove how we love God,
We're supplied with good news quite reversed.

(The limerick form probably comes from County Limerick in Ireland, and thus is the form here, near St. Patrick's Day.)

Romans 5:1–11

The Way Forward

Since we are justified by faith,
We now have peace, through Christ, with God;
Can you believe that someone died
So you might know, though being odd,
You're even loved more than you thought?
I do not "get" we're saved from wrath;
But if some gratitude I learn,
Then that will do—and be my path.

THE FOURTH SUNDAY IN LENT (A)—
1 SAMUEL 16:1-13; JOHN 9:1-41

1 Samuel 16:1-13

The Name of the Program

How curious we have the names
Of three who did not fit the claim
That one of Jesse's sons would be
The king, by Yahweh "designeed."

Thus, Samuel has to turn away
Eliab, who, though he displayed
The stature of some handsome king,
Had not the heart from which grace springs.

Nor Abinadab, nor Shammah
Elicited some grand "Aha!"
From Samuel, nor the other four
Would be where Yahweh's spirit poured.

But by this boy did Yahweh name
His program, which we still proclaim:
You never know, despite your plans,
Where love for you, and all, might land.

John 9:1–41

Sight

John says the man was blind from birth,
Which means they thought he had a dearth
Of goodness, or, perhaps his parents
Were the ones who had been errant—
For otherwise, who can explain
Conditions we find inhumane?

But Jesus isn't into reasons,
Or int'rested in open season
On those calamity befalls;
Instead, his actions always call
Attention to the acts of God
We find so hard to see, and odd.

If anything, let him remind
Us if we miss God's love, we're blind.

THE FIFTH SUNDAY IN LENT (A)—
EZEKIEL 37:1–14 AND JOHN 11:1–45

God Enamored

"O mortal, can these dead bones live?"
"O Lord, my God, you know;"
I wonder which came first—the trust
Ezekiel, despite woe,
Embodied? Or—the vision, which
Appeared, and made him brave
Enough he might proclaim the news
That Yahweh yet would save?

And which comes first, belief in Christ,
So, dying, one still lives?
Or—when you've seen the hopeless, change—
Know God enamored gives?
Perhaps it doesn't matter how
From death you might come out,
Just listen to Love's call, who still
By grace, all dying flouts.

(The phrase "God enamored gives" is from a poem by Robert Louis Stevenson, "Come, My Beloved, Hear from Me.")

PALM SUNDAY, LITURGY OF THE PALMS (A)— PSALM 118:1-2, 19-29; MATTHEW 21:1-11

Psalm 118:1–2, 19–29

Our Parentage

O Church! Do not forget our parentage,
Our roots in Israel of old;
Our parents cried "Hosanna" to the LORD,
A plea to save—and now! So bold
Were they, they cried it yet again that day
When Jesus rode his donkey in,
While from the city's other side, the king—
Who did not save—with pomp and din
Of horse and armor tried to claim the power
That oft has captured human hearts;
But in this fam'ly tree we've seen a love
Passed down which still is off the charts.

Matthew 21:1–11

The Donkey in the Room

We like to keep our politics
Apart from Sunday church;
And woe to preachers who would dare
The worship to besmirch
With commentary on the powers
That tend to rule the day;
And yes, it can be overdone—
And peoples' trust betray;
But Jesus, on parade that day,
Lampooned the power and might
Of all, like Caesar, who in great
Display would take delight;
He's making fun of those who lord
It over people's hearts;
This Jesus, not just meek and mild,
Is brave, and heav'nly smart.

RESURRECTION OF THE LORD (A)—
MATTHEW 28:1-10

Resurrection Key

A choral work, in major key,
The Bach *Magnificat in D*,
Once made me laugh out loud to hear
Repeated music, that appeared
Within the Gloria Patri when
The music came around again—
As it was *in the beginning*!
Clever Bach had, in our singing,
Taken us to where we'd started,
Scoring notes already charted.
This technique which Bach employed
Elicits, it turns out, much joy.

So, Matthew, cleverness displayed
With Jesus' "Do not be afraid;
Tell [them] to go to Galilee;
[For it is] there they will see me."
Why Galilee? It's at the start!
And there it is you'll find the heart
Of who the risen Jesus is—
In all the things he did then, viz.,
Forgiving, healing, and inviting—
It makes this risen Lord exciting
Since you can see him there, today—
And Resurrection, thus convey.

Go back, the story read anew,
May then his life repeat in you.

(The idea that "Galilee" means going back to the beginning of Matthew's Gospel comes
from Tom Long in *The Christian Century*, April 4, 2006.)

THE SECOND SUNDAY OF EASTER (A)—
JOHN 20:19–31; 1 PETER 1:3–9

John 20:19–31

Your door's too light to shut out God.

Young man—
Young woman—
Old man—
Old woman—
Middle-aged man—
Middle-aged woman—
Your door's too light to shut out God.
You may think
You're safe from trouble
And nothing can get in,
You may think
The door is barred
For fear of what has been,
You may think
That what you've done could
Never be forgiven,
Or most of all,
That love is gone,
Along with joyful living;
But when for all
That you've been through
You then expect the least,
The Lord of love
Will walk right in
And say just one word: Peace.

(The beginning is a take-off on James Weldon Johnson's "The Prodigal Son" from *God's Trombones*.)

1 Peter 1:3–9

*Quasimodogeniti Sunday**

As in the style of newborn babes
We do not know what's yet to come;
Believers, by the world's strong powers
May, like our Lord, be yet undone;
And yet, there's more that's up God's sleeve,
An unformed hope by which we live,
It cannot be imagined; yet,
We trust the one who gives and gives.

Such trust is what will save our souls,
In gladness, now, our God extol!

(*Name given to this day because of the traditional introit's text (in Latin) from
1 Peter 2:2: "Like newborn infants (*Quasi modo géniti infántes*) long for the pure, spiri-
tual milk, so that by it you may grow into salvation." This poem was also inspired by an
interview with Bishop Thomas of the Coptic Orthodox Church of Al-Quosia, Upper
Egypt, at http://www.presbyterianmission.org/story/carrying-cross-without-fear/.)

THE THIRD SUNDAY OF EASTER (A)—
ACTS 2:14a, 36–41; LUKE 24:13–35

Acts 2:14a, 36–41

Drop in the Bucket

It's almost like an afterthought,
The number who were added.
Before, the news that Jesus was
Messiah had been dreaded
Because, if he was dead and gone,
From whence would come their rescue?
What kind of gratitude was that,
To crucify, not thank, you?

Thus, at a crossroads did they find
Themselves, while Pete exhorted;
And heard God's reach extended wide,
And could not be distorted
To say that just a few could reap
The benefits of living
With knowledge of the God who made
A name by faithful giving.

But now, all immigrants to faith
Were welcomed without papers,
For Christ, in giving all, had waived
Restrictions on their neighbors;
Three thousand, in the bucket, then,
Was just a drop's beginning
Toward when a world with love for all
Will one day sure be brimming.

Luke 24:13–35

In the Breaking

This long and detailed story makes
It seem as if the writer knew
First hand "what things" took place that day
When Cleopas, and other Jews,
Recounted to this stranger how
"Their" leaders had turned Jesus in;
If Luke was there, then even he
Can't recognize the man as kin!
And even after teaching—words
You'd think that they would recognize—
It's only in the breaking of
The bread, the Lord is now reprised;
This breaking—word made flesh—by one
Born in the place called house of bread,
Is how in each and ev'ry age
We'll see him risen from the dead.

THE FOURTH SUNDAY OF EASTER (A)—
ACTS 2:42–47; 1 PETER 2:19–25

Acts 2:42–47

The Devotee

They devoted themselves to the teaching served up
By the apostles and each others' care,
They devoted themselves in the power of love,
To the breaking of bread and the prayers;
These two words, "they devoted," now fill me with awe;
What a gift that such zeal they had!
What a wonder that all were provided with what
They had need of, which made them all glad!
And not just in the temple was church, then, "the church,"
But 'twas even at home as they ate,
Where their generous hearts and their genuine praise
All the peoples' goodwill did create;
Not by effort or work did community grow
To the faith that we now still can see,
But from all that would keep us from joy are we saved
By the Lord, who's the first devotee.

1 Peter 2:19–25

Threshold

It's quite a puzzle, isn't it,
How by his wounds you have been healed?
It says "from sins," but what is that?
Some basic human law repealed—
The law that says each person fears
To lose what he or she has gained,
One's safety, wealth, or way of life,
The things you've worked hard to attain?
The way you have to grasp for more,
Sometimes, no matter what the cost?
But then some person gives his all—
It's like a threshold has been crossed,
Some door into a life that's free
From worry since this person gave,
Without a thought for self—and now
You, too, can act as one who's saved.

THE FIFTH SUNDAY OF EASTER (A)—
ACTS 7:55-60; JOHN 14:1-14

Acts 7:55–60

Prelude to a Fall

Who knows if Saul, in seeing Stephen's faith so strange,
Was set to wond'ring if he simply was deranged,
Or if forgiveness was some quality divine
In Jesus that, in Stephen, had life redefined?
I think he wondered, as he pondered what to do,
If all his zeal was misplaced, which next construed
A twinge of doubt in what he'd been, 'long with remorse,
Which then portended being knocked right off his horse.

John 14:1–14

Way, Truth, and Life

I am the way, and I am the truth;
I am the life by which you may live;
Let no one say that for God to be real,
One must utter God's name; then God will give.
"Is that what I said? Oh no! Read the text!
Right! It's my *way*, how I *lived* that's the key;
My goal is never to make folks perplexed,
But if you live my way, surely you'll see
The Father who lives in me, living in you!
You'll have all you need; all you ask will come through."

THE SIXTH SUNDAY OF EASTER (A)—
ACTS 17:22-31; JOHN 14:15-21

Acts 17:22–31

Oh, What a Politician!

Oh, what a politician,
Is Paul among the Greeks!
He says they are religious,
Who e'en unknown gods seek;
And then with news he hits them:
The God who made all things
Lives not in what's made by us—
Our wealth, our fame, our bling—
But we, in fact (per poets
They knew) are God's offspring!
Which means the highest value
Of which we all can sing,
Is: Love, like of a parent,
Defines our life and death;
May Jesus be our policy
With every daily breath.

John 14:15–21

If You Love Me

"If you love me,
keep my commandments,
And I will pray the Father,
And he will give you
another Comforter."

"You're not alone,
When you keep my words,
(He says that it's forever!)
You sure have it made,
Since the Spirit's with you."

"Because I live,
You will live also
(How many times I've said that!)
Father, Son, Spirit—
Enough love all around!"

(The poem's meter is a bit unusual: 4/5/7/5/6. Jesus' opening words pretty much determined it. Maybe his words determining things is how it should be all the time for us!)

THE ASCENSION OF THE LORD/THE SEVENTH SUNDAY OF EASTER (A)—
ACTS 1:6-14; LUKE 24:44-53

Acts 1:6-14

Ascendit in Coelum

They must have thought that they had failed
When, strung up on the cross and nailed,
He died, with all he'd giv'n, undone,
The end of all their joy now come.

But then, they briefly knew him there!
In upper room and beach, despair
Dissolved! How could it be, I ask,
That Love returned, with death unmasked
As powerless his end to make?

I know not how, nor could they take
This joy for granted, for he soon
Rose out of sight, while they, marooned,
Stood open-mouthed at such a turn,
Hopes dashed again, until they yearned
For his return; Now, more than twelve,
This fam'ly with their fears dissolved,
Are gathered, back in upper room,
This birthplace of the church, this womb,
Where soon, in eating, prayer, and hymn,
By Spirit, they'll be born again.

Luke 24:44–53

From Stressing to Blessing

Luke's first book ends with the ascension;
Without much fanfare, his attention
Not focused high, is on the promise:
"He said that there would come upon us
The power on high that's from the Father
That we might tell the news much farther
From here in town than we'd imagined!"
So thus, when what we now know, happened,
They had his words in their back pockets,
Until they'd come out from the closet
When they had dealt with all their stressing
By worshiping the God of blessings.

THE DAY OF PENTECOST (A)—ACTS 2:1-21

A Brief History of Bulgaria
or
Ode on a Thracian Urn

The Thracians with their works of gold,
And then Bulgarians of old,
The Byzantines of Empire East,
Then Bulgars once again increased,
Then people under Turkish "yoke"
(A word old hatred still evokes)
Revival that was long delayed,
Turks overthrown with Russian aid,
A culture trying to transpose
Until the Communists imposed
A system that would steal the hearts
Of each one's worth and diff'ring arts.

Oh, can a country grow in pride
When hist'ry o'er the years decries
First one group, then again, another,
Believing only blood makes brothers?
Oh, can God's Spirit work its power,
Not by religion, but by showers
Of truth and hope and understanding?
And can we all, our love expanding,
Perceive with empathy each child
Of God, who on the world still smiles?
Oh, let us put our racial pride
And fear, and wrongs, and guilt aside
And work like heav'n to make a world
Where flags of love are e'er unfurled.

Oh, What Would They Do?

A sound like the rush of a violent wind
Filled the whole house with all of them there;
These tongues, or this *ruach*, this fire, appeared,
Like an answer to all of their prayers;
Oh, what would they do, with their Lord up and gone,
Out of sight, vanished, gone, disappeared?
Thus, fire from heaven, like Sinai encore,
All their doubts of the kingdom then cleared:
The news of salvation is not some obscure
Or exclusive thing meant for a few;
All manner of folk, of all nations on earth
Now are given the love that makes new.

TRINITY SUNDAY (A)—
GENESIS 1:1-2:4a; MATTHEW 28:16-20

Genesis 1:1-2:4a

Creation Boiled Down

First, when chaos reigns and life is ruined,
There will always be light;
Second, when we find ourselves lost and at sea,
There is yet air to breathe;
Third, when we are flailing around thinking there is no tomorrow,
There are still grounds for planting trees and tilling gardens;
Fourth, when we are completely under the weather,
The sun and the moon will rise;
Fifth, when we feel like a fish out of water, with bird brains,
We really don't have to be everything to everybody;
Sixth, when we think it's all about us,
There are countless other creatures, but we're made to create;
Seventh, when we think we have to work until we drop,
Even God said, "I've gotta get out of the office."

Man, that's good!

(Walter Brueggemann used the line about God getting out of the office in a talk I heard many years ago.)

Matthew 28:16–20

His Face, Everywhere

Sometimes it seems most of my Facebook feeds
Are full of rants and diatribes and screeds
That, I admit, all have their point that we
Must pay attention, and not fail to see
Injustice wheresoever it might lie,
Not be complacent, ills of the world deny.
And yet, I also know that I need more
Than simply outrage over sin abhorred.

Be angry, yes, but then never forget
The time they worshiped, and some doubted, yet
He told them that despite the wrong they'd known,
Authority o'er all was his alone;
Which means his way, his grace, his love, his face
Can never be supplanted or replaced
By anyone or anything; so sing,
Since his enduring life is one sure thing.

THE ELEVENTH SUNDAY IN ORDINARY TIME/
SECOND AFTER PENTECOST (A)—
GENESIS 18:1-15, 21:1-7

Oh, Abraham!

Oh, Abraham! You run to greet
Three strangers who come down the street;
You bow to them, and then entreat
Them come inside that they might eat.
What moves you, that you so reveal
Extravagance, as next you kneel
To wash their feet, and bid them rest,
As if by gracious acts you're blessed?

And then another blessing from
The visitors, while Sarah, mum,
By door, to laughter still succumbs,
Since it's as if the kingdom's come.
Oh, joy! Though how they'll fare's unknown,
The promise still is ne'er outgrown;
And gospel even yet ensues
To those who hospitality pursue.

THE TWELFTH SUNDAY IN ORDINARY TIME/
THIRD AFTER PENTECOST (A)—GENESIS 21:8-21
AND MATTHEW 10:24-39; ROMANS 6:1b-11

Genesis 21:8-21 and Matthew 10:24-39

Expressions of Faith

The fat was in the fire
When Isaac and Ishmael played;
The pot just boiled over
With Sarah, for Isaac afraid;
The mother lost it then—
The father saw no way to win;
He couldn't stand the heat,
So Abraham had to give in;
I wonder if he knew
He'd cast his burden on the Lord
When casting Hagar out
To sink or swim of her accord?
The death sentence he gave,
He pushed to the back of his mind;
This tale thus goes to show
The love of this Yahweh is blind;
For all concerned were saved,
And saw the Lord does not slumber;
Or put another way—
The hairs of your head are all numbered.

(The first line, from Frederick Buechner's writing about Hagar in *Peculiar Treasures* [Harper & Row, 1979] and the subsequent *Beyond Words*, inspired the poem.)

Romans 6:1b–11

Wonder

I have to hope that no one wonders
If too much sin of theirs can sunder
From them the possibilities of grace
When feeling like a real basket case!
For grace is nothing theoretical,
Nor would it ever tilt heretical
To say that all who want to know it
Can have the life Christ spent to show it.
His resurrection's no reward
For upright living you might hoard;
Dear wonder man and woman, it cuts through
For you. Who's freed. Right now. Out of the blue.

THE THIRTEENTH SUNDAY IN ORDINARY TIME/ FOURTH AFTER PENTECOST (A)— GENESIS 22:1–14; MATTHEW 10:40–42

Genesis 22:1–14

"Here I Am"

Three times he says those faithful words,
Which says, what is its own reward
Is something so courageous, bold
(And hardly what we're often told),
That anyone who dares to set
Foot in a church should plan to get
Assaulted by the task at hand!
This, "Here I am," or "Here I stand,"
As Luther said more recently,
Means trust beyond what we can see,
Not knowing how or when or where
Your actions will God's grace declare.

Matthew 10:40–42

Remembering Jesus on a Hot One

So, this Sunday, you could turn off the sanctuary's A.C.
Or, you northerners who don't have it, keep the windows closed.
Put a sign on each one: "Windows need to stay closed today."
Hope that it's a hot one.
Let the people start to grumble, at least to themselves.
And then after this text is read, ask everyone to think
Of someone they consider to be a true disciple of Jesus,
Living or dead, famous or just a neighbor they know.
Then lots of elders and/or deacons come forward
Carrying trays filled with cups of cold water (not lukewarm!)
And as if they're passing out the Sacrament,
They pass the tray to the people on the ends of the pews,
Saying, "I give you this cold water in the name of _____."
The trays get passed down the row, with each person saying,
"I give you this cold water in the name of _____."
And lots of disciples of Jesus will be named aloud.
And lots of Christ's little ones will have their thirsts quenched.
It'll be cool. They'll remember it.
Maybe they'll remember Jesus, too.

THE FOURTEENTH SUNDAY IN ORDINARY TIME/ FIFTH AFTER PENTECOST (A)—GENESIS 24:34– 38, 42–49, 58–67; MATTHEW 11:16–19, 25–30

Genesis 24:34–38, 42–49, 58–67

Toto, We're Not in Kansas Anymore

These days, we might call it racist,
Sending for a bride for your son
Back home amongst your own people;
So what's wrong with Canaanite girls?

I sit in a local restaurant,
Amazed at combinations here,
Black and white, and Asian and white,
And the new grandparents who aren't
(I surmise) entirely happy
With their white daughter's non-white spouse;
It's a new world, to some's chagrin,
But I think: This is wonderful.

Abraham needed son Isaac
Not to forsake this new Yahweh;
But much more than race was at stake—
Much more than he could imagine.

God cares not a whit about tribe,
But only what it takes to see
What someday all will know: Just love
Is what defines our family tree.

Matthew 11:16–19, 25–30

The News beyond Comparing

It isn't hard to picture
The children in this scripture
Because we know how childish
It is, and sometimes stylish,
To rant and rave whenever
It seems some new endeavor
Will rock the boat we're sailing,
And set us all awailing.

Thus John provoked despising,
And Jesus, moralizing;
But Jesus knew that infants,
Without the world's enrichments,
Know only their receiving,
Which boils down to believing
That one thing never changes:
The love which he arranges.

THE FIFTEENTH SUNDAY IN ORDINARY TIME/
SIXTH AFTER PENTECOST (A)—
GENESIS 25:19-34; MATTHEW 13:1-9, 18-23;
ROMANS 8:1-11

Genesis 25:19-34

Poor Isaac

Scarred for life by that trip up Moriah,
His father tries to make it up to him
By getting a girl for him from back home.
But like father, like son, and the wife can't conceive.
Like father, like son, and the promise is in jeopardy.
Like father like son, and young Isaac tries to pass off his wife.
Like father, like son, and old Isaac prays.
And now a new wrinkle—twins,
And the right of the first-born out the window!
A dullard and a grabber, hardly the best of friends;
Father and mother each with their own favorite.

I'll bet it wasn't what old Isaac had in mind.
I hope one day he had the last laugh.

Matthew 13:1–9, 18–23

The Happy Sower

We misconstrue this parable
To say where people fail
To let the word take hold, as if—
"Oh God! It won't prevail
Without more folk like us—good soil—
To make a healthy yield!"
Except—this sower's joy's so full,
The point is not the field,
But that he flings it everywhere,
And that he won't hold back;
"Huzzah!" (It's there!) "Hurray!" (And there!),
With each dip in his sack;
Think back four weeks to Genesis,
Day one, day two, day three,
God throwing out things here and there,
"That's good!" he cries with glee!
Thus by the sea our Lord assures
The crowd all gathered there—
And all of us—to know again,
That way beyond compare,
Are all the possibilities
Created by this sower,
Just take it in, and it will grow,
Because of this grace thrower.

Romans 8:1–11

"He condemned sin in the flesh"

Oh, which did God in Christ condemn?
The sins we know so well, in them—
That is, in others not like us—
Or in ourselves, which make less fuss?

Or is it not those sins themselves,
But maybe God in Christ rebels
Against the notion that sins "count"
Against some magical amount
That at love's bar would cut you off?
("No more for you!")
                                        To that, God scoffs.

The mind that's still set on the flesh,
That is, on me, just doesn't mesh
With what the law of love can do;
Love throws the system all askew.
For neither doing nor believing
Is any match for your receiving.

THE SIXTEENTH SUNDAY IN ORDINARY TIME/
SEVENTH AFTER PENTECOST (A)—
GENESIS 28:10–19a; ROMANS 8:12–25

Genesis 28:12–19a

This Stairway to Heaven Really Makes Me Wonder

"How awesome is this place," he says,
Where hope and presence intersect;
It is as if God lives where, missing
What you long for, you expect
It yet to be!
Though you can't see
What otherwise would leave you stunned;
And so the LORD to Jacob says,
"I will not leave you 'til I've done
What I have promised."
So, I ask,
Does this mean God might someday leave?
The text implies as much!
And yet,
Perhaps God's "present" when we cleave
To what, in hope, we cannot see,
And God's house—Bethel—is that place
And time when you and everyone
Now realize an awesome grace
Is—more than moon and heaven—ours,
And stairways climb to more than stars.

Romans 8:12–25

This Much Is Clear

I worry where the world is headed,
With climate change not only dreaded,
But now a chunk the size of Delaware
Has broken from Antarctica. Beware!

I worry that, back home, the President,
—By tweets and, what he says, the evidence,
Non-curious, and with a one-track mind—
Cares just for money, sex, his base and kind.

He has no understanding of us all;
But kings and rulers often have appalled
The people they are meant by God to serve;
We do not always get what we deserve.

And so, although in pain creation groans,
A God of love can ne'er despair condone;
Since hope in Christ's the opposite of fear,
His people, still, can daily make it clear.

Genesis 29:15–28

Holy Fools

The cheat became the cheated,
In Laban he met his match;
To marry Laban's daughters off,
A daring plan was hatched;
When Jacob saw those lovely eyes,
He knew that he'd been had,
His eyes were opened to the truth:
"I'm not the only cad!"
I wonder if the "girls" were in on
Laban's crafty plan?
He says, "*We'll* give the other, too,
If you serve *me* [the man]
Another set of seven years."
Thus, he whose mother pulled
The wool over his father's eyes,
By women, too, was fooled!
Oh! What a pack of fools and foolers
Form this family tree!
Which goes to show the nature of
The prodigality
Behind the LORD who chose them all
As blessers and as blessed;
And holy fools today still know
By love they are possessed.

Romans 8:26–39

No Magic

How odd our sacred book admits
We often don't know how to pray,
And yet, how wonderful, in Christ
There are no magic words to say.

No special turn of phrase is key
To what's profound, unlocked within,
No need to speak at all, in fact,
No *should* or *ought*, no promised spin.

For God's the one who now conspires
For good with those whose love is prayer,
A company, a family
Whose glory is beyond compare.

The reason why, cannot be proved,
Explained in sermon or in poem,
Not words, but just the fact of love
Is how the One who counts is known.

THE EIGHTEENTH SUNDAY IN ORDINARY TIME/
NINTH AFTER PENTECOST (A)—
GENESIS 32:22-31 AND MATTHEW 14:13-21;
ROMANS 9:1-5

Genesis 32:22–31 and Matthew 14:13–21

Hilarious Unexpectedness

It's as if, like his grandfather,
He, too, plays a game of chicken
With this Yahweh, testing whether
He can entrust all that he has
To the promise of abundance;
He sends them off, unprotected,
Wrestling all night with what he's done.
But the grabber gets a blessing,
Although it doesn't come scot-free—
Faith limps in this, our family tree.

Along comes Jesus. He's alone;
In his own way, he's wrestling, too.
The crowds can't get enough of him;
Can his disciples carry on?
But they need another lesson—
Astonishing numbers he feeds!
Hilarious unexpectedness,
Not disaster we expect,
Is news that comes again this week,
When of this God, we dare to speak.

(The phrase "hilarious unexpectedness" is from Frederick Buechner, *Telling the Truth: The Gospel as Comedy, Tragedy, and Fairy Tale* [HarperOne, 1977].)

Romans 9:1–5

Original Testament to Grace

Oh, would more Christians viewed the "Old"
More like "Original," extolled
Just like the "New," a testament
To gospel, with the temperament
Of all the grace you find in Paul;
Although his people weren't enthralled
By Christ, it works the other way
Around, for Christians oft betray
The faith in which our Lord was raised.
Instead of *old*, dare be amazed
At how *original* and *new*
Is love by which our forebears grew.
—And so can you.

THE NINETEENTH SUNDAY IN ORDINARY TIME/
TENTH AFTER PENTECOST (A)—
GENESIS 37:1-28 [5-11 OFFICIALLY NOT
INCLUDED]; MATTHEW 14:22-33

Genesis 37:1-28

Another "Here I Am!"

Once again you have to wonder
If a patriarch believes—
For Jacob knows the boys can't stand
This Joseph with long sleeves;
It's not as if the father is
Oblivious to the threat;
He knows how much the dreamer is
Despised by them—And yet
He still sends out his pride and joy
(Another lamb to slaughter);
He knows the opportunity
Will make their mouths all water!
I think deep down he wonders: "Is
This promise true? Or tale?"
Is this a challenge to the LORD
To see if it will fail?
Perhaps his father, Isaac, once
Had told him 'bout that ram,
Then, just like Grandpa, Joseph tells
His father, "Here I am!"
It takes all kinds to grow this faith,
The doubters and the brave;
The truth is, Yahweh works through both
To show the love that saves.

(Please see also the poem for the Thirteenth Sunday in Ordinary Time/Fourth after Pentecost about the almost-sacrifice of Isaac.)

Matthew 14:22–33

Just a Bit

He makes them go into the boat,
And while he prays, to go ahead;
He tells them not to be afraid—
Unlike a ghost, he isn't dead;
To Peter, he commands he come
To him atop the batt'ring waves;
He notes that Peter has some faith,
And some is all it takes to save;
But some was not enough for Pete,
Who thought that he should have it all.
If that's your goal, then you're all wet,
A bit of trust avoids a fall.

THE TWENTIETH SUNDAY IN ORDINARY TIME/
ELEVENTH AFTER PENTECOST (A)—
GENESIS 45:1-15; MATTHEW 15:(10-20), 21-28

Genesis 45:1-15

"And after this his brothers talked with him."

I wonder what it was they talked about
When Joseph finally told them who he was?
Perhaps, "How's Dinah? How's she holding up?"
Or, "How's your mother?" "Yours?" "And yours?" because
We're led to think he cared about such things;
We can guess, "Don't be angry with yourselves"
Reveals he knew his family well enough
To see that deep within these brothers twelve
Was worry over whom Dad loved the best!
He later* tells them not to quarrel on the way.
They talked. They left. The promise did not die;
And talk is not as cheap as people say.

*(vs. 24)

Matthew 15:(10–20) 21–28

It's the Canaanite Woman Who Gives Me Delight

Oh, to think that he learned it from some Canaanite,
When he knew it quite well, but he wasn't quite right;
When he argued how food couldn't make you defiled,
Which in hearing reports, made the Pharisees riled,
Since to toss out religion, tradition, and rules
Can produce people fearful and fretful and fools!
But the prophets have always decried when a rite
Has, in hurting the poor, turned creative thought, trite;
Jesus, too, observed how the establishment fails
To point out where a lot of, quote, "goodness" oft ails;
But he found himself mouthing some "tried and true" aims
That did nothing the love of his God to proclaim:
Thus, the Canaanite mom played her prophetic role,
Reaching back to Hosea and Amos and Joel;
But the thing about Jesus is, he paid her heed—
Helping those who now follow him, follow her lead!

THE TWENTY-FIRST SUNDAY IN ORDINARY TIME/TWELFTH AFTER PENTECOST (A)— EXODUS 1:8–2:10; MATTHEW 16:13–20

Exodus 1:8–2:10

Five Women's Disobedience

The civil disobedience
Of women isn't new,
Nor did it stop with just one case
Where midwives helped push through
The life that Yahweh had in mind;
Oh, no! This kind of birth,
Meant not for just a few back then
Is all about the worth
Of all—despite some despot's claim
That he could cleanse a race
Right off the map! His daughter even
Risks her own disgrace,
While Shiphrah and Puah, and Moses'
Mother and sister, too,
By their outwitting, show this LORD
Will never be subdued.

Matthew 16:13–20

"Then he sternly ordered the disciples not to tell anyone that he was the Messiah."

Perhaps he thought a movement, underground,
Would be more fitting for his church
Than something popular, and much renowned;
Who knows? The Lord, I guess. But search
The scriptures and you'll see it's hard to find
Cathedrals, or a meetinghouse,
Or power, or wealth; for what this Peter binds,
Is us to Christ, despite our doubts,
Faced every day, that he alone can save;
We're free to follow him—we're loosed!—
In church or out; but in, are people brave,
Because from love they're ne'er seduced.

(It may well be that the terms "bind" and "loose" are rabbinic for forbidding and permitting, but here I see the former as forbidding our separation from God and the latter as permitting us to follow in the footsteps of the Lord of all.)

THE TWENTY-SECOND SUNDAY IN ORDINARY TIME/THIRTEENTH AFTER PENTECOST (A)— EXODUS 3:1–15; MATTHEW 16:21–28

Exodus 3:1–15

When God Notices

So Moses, just a shepherd in the wilderness,
Whose job, to watch for sheep that might be in distress,
Observes an unconsumed, yet burning bush one day,
And does not think it better that he stay away!
Instead, he turns aside to see this bush in flames,
And from the bush, the LORD twice calls out Moses' name
Upon the LORD's observing that this Moses looked!
How strange that Moses does not think his goose is cooked,
But like his forebears, Abraham and Isaac, too,
And Jacob (even Esau!) says words like, "I do."

This *Here I am*'s a sign of danger up ahead,
As if, through thick and thin, the speaker then is wed
To One whose promise not a bed of roses gives,
But, rather, presence, if the speaker dares to live
As if this LORD rests not, until oppression ends;
Perhaps, this means, you'll be the one this see-er sends;
He calls himself, to Moses, I AM WHO I AM,
And adds the name, the LORD, the God of Abraham,
The God of Isaac, and the God of Jacob, too.
And holiness is more than taking off your shoes.

Matthew 16:21–28

Special Agents

Sometimes it almost seems as if
Another person pushes him
To go where he has not yet gone,
Such as the Canaanite, who showed
That she was not some dog, when with
Her grace and wit she took him on;
And now, with Peter's push against
His telling them about his fate,
He pushes harder back to say
Not only he, but even those
Who follow him should be prepared
Their cross to take—it's now *their* way.

The heroes of this holy book
Are never fixed, are never still;
They bend, they move, and even Jesus
Bends to do his Father's will.

THE TWENTY-THIRD SUNDAY IN ORDINARY TIME/FOURTEENTH AFTER PENTECOST (A)— EXODUS 12:1–14; MATTHEW 18:15–20

Exodus 12:1–14

Know How to Party!

This text, combining liturgy
And narrative in one,
Things like, "You shall" plus "I'll pass over"
Say that we're not done
With any biblical "account"
Until we realize,
What makes it sacred is when we,
Somehow, internalize
The things that happened way back when.
Thus, in our time and place,
The story's meant to give to us
A measure of the grace
That we still need, that is, the news
That God's the one who saves
From slavery, disaster; and,
From cradle to the grave
Will not abandon you, so thus,
Don't fail or hesitate,
Within your households everywhere,
Such love to celebrate.

Matthew 18:15–20

Ouch!

In case you think that Jesus gave us rules
That we can use to run the church, some tools
For how to deal with disagreement;
Or how, in anyone's community,
The way to solve all that disunity
Is give the worst the kicked-out treatment—
Remember how he treated tax collectors,
Or people over in the gentile sector,
And love them even more than it's convenient!

THE TWENTY-FOURTH SUNDAY IN ORDINARY TIME/FIFTEENTH AFTER PENTECOST (A)— EXODUS 14:19-31; MATTHEW 18:21-35

Exodus 14:19–31

Dead on the Seashore

This text, awash in vividness,
Reveals the LORD's omnipotence,
But maybe not in how it seems;
It's not just that the waters cleared,
But that the LORD here persevered
To see the still enslaved, redeemed.

The program of this one we laud
Is less that we, the act applaud,
And more we're grounded in the why:
God always stands with those oppressed,
While those who cause others' distress
God with a mighty arm, defies.

Matthew 18:21–35

For Your Own Good

Beware the preacher who pontificates,
The one who has to tell the people what to do;
Beware bad news, when we are in bad straits:
"Forgiveness is the thing to which we all must hew
Or else!" For though the text appears to say
That God is like a king who'll throw you into jail—
Who, if you don't forgive, will make you pay—
If Jesus said it, he means evil will prevail
Within our hearts, 'cause that's the way things are!
It's how God made it; enmity will eat away,
Forever burning, evermore to scar,
Until its hold by you is loosed; and that's the day
When you discover that what God holds dear
Is you! Forgiveness is what puts *you* in the clear.

THE TWENTY-FIFTH SUNDAY IN ORDINARY TIME/SIXTEENTH AFTER PENTECOST (A)— EXODUS 16:2–15 AND MATTHEW 20:1–16

Manna (For Late Workers, Too)

They said, "What is it?" each to each,
For they did not know what it was;

(Some workers, the owner beseeched
With their clear but self-righteous cause);

The kingdom's hard to recognize,
Though it be in front of our nose;

(The generous Giver defies
When we think we know how things go);

We never know when we might see
New gifts rained right down on our heads;

(Others, too, have had answered pleas:
"Give us this day our daily bread");

To you it will come, and to all,
And each and all hungers erase;

(The last will be first, the first last,
Surprise is the hallmark of grace.)

THE TWENTY-SIXTH SUNDAY IN ORDINARY TIME/SEVENTEENTH AFTER PENTECOST (A)— EXODUS 17:1–7; MATTHEW 21:23–32

Exodus 17:1–7

Is the LORD Among Us or Not?

Is the LORD among us or not?
Is a question everyone's asked,
In the face of suffering and pain,
When by loss and grief you're harassed.

When life sucks, and death hits your gut,
It's so clear that God is no more;
Just mentioning God seems absurd—
Until there's a knock at the door.

There, a neighbor friend has come by,
And with kindness touches your heart,
Uninvited, out of the blue,
You taste what this Moses imparts.

And you've found you won't die of thirst,
And for now, you really believe,
For the best of love is the kind
That by grace you've simply received.

Matthew 21:23–32

Brand New: Not Just a Slogan Anymore

Since, if anyone is in Christ,
There's a new creation—
Since the past is finished and gone,
And everything's brand new—
There's no need not to change your mind!
Old convictions don't count,
Don't worry about precedents,
Don't worry you'll look weak,
Who you are today is what counts;
Maybe you were dead wrong,
Or maybe even partly right,
But that was then, before;
And God is not above getting
Down on hands and knees to
Bring the least of us around to
The here and now of love.

THE TWENTY-SEVENTH SUNDAY IN ORDINARY TIME/EIGHTEENTH AFTER PENTECOST (A)— EXODUS 20:1-4, 7-9, 12-20; MATTHEW 21:33-46

Exodus 20:1–4, 7–9, 12–20

Ten Little Words

These words, so old, are easy to ignore
Because we think they bear the force of Law,
(As thought by people like that Judge Roy Moore
Suspended—twice—because his thinking's flawed!)
While we, the church, are people who think grace
Implies God does not tell us what to do.
And yet these words are one more classic case
Revealing One whose passion still breaks through.

For these "commandments" simply say what's true
About a way of life that's good for all;
It's mostly common sense that's so construed
By holy writ, in hopes it might forestall
Our self-destructive acts which jeopardize
Community! Because deep down, God yearns
Such rules might save this human enterprise,
Till love for all, from God, we might discern.

Matthew 21:33–46

The Landowner

Our view of God's so saccharine
We shrink from such a God where sin
Results in consequence! So hence,
We think this tale's about the Jews
Who, like those tenants, didn't choose
To follow Jesus, but instead
Made sure that he'd be silenced—dead!

But what if all this violence
Is in itself the great offense,
Where not just Jews, but those in pews
And pulpit, too, can be ensnared,
If ever all our wealth we dare
To think is ours! And we refuse
To think that God is owed God's dues?

God's mercy is forever sure,
Not just for those who think they're pure,
And God can offer all God owns
To all who thought they were disowned.

THE TWENTY-EIGHTH SUNDAY IN ORDINARY TIME/NINETEENTH AFTER PENTECOST (A)— EXODUS 32:1–14 (15–20); MATTHEW 22:1–14

Exodus 32:1–14 (15–20)

Unforgettable Reading

She must have been just eight years old,
I asked her if she'd read that day;
Her voice, so strong and so controlled,
I hear it in my mind's replay
(An octave higher than 'tis now)
It woke the people up, so clear!
With bold expression, furrowed brow,
Her Moses pleads the LORD might hear,
And change his mind! But grace not cheap,
Her rising voice described the scene
Of reveling and dancers' leaps,
And Moses, hot—not church serene!—
With tablets smashed—and calf all burned—
To powder, ground—and then in rage—
The most bizarre—how Israel learned
No idol can our thirst assuage!

I love the passion of that day;
No age can take such faith away.

(Dedicated to Lindsay Ann Barton Cassidy)

Matthew 22:1–14

Looking Like a Million Dollars

I'm not sure how the punishment
Described by Jesus fits the crime—
The killing and the burning here
Should not be told in children's time!
But those who will not recognize
The lavish gift of every day
Are doomed to miss the best of life,
And find themselves, in time, dismayed.

It's not so much the underdressed
Wore shorts, say, but that they were short
On caring for why they'd been called,
And thus, God's purposes would thwart;
In Christ's an invitation to
A life that's clothed by love, transformed
So that your heart is made anew,
And, garbed with grace for all, your norm.

THE TWENTY-NINTH SUNDAY IN ORDINARY TIME/TWENTIETH AFTER PENTECOST (A)— EXODUS 33:12-23; MATTHEW 22:15-22

Exodus 33:12-23

The Conversation

Moses keeps upping the ante,
He asks the LORD for more and more.
Though it seems this LORD knows his name—
What are your ways? How keep favor?
(Besides they're *your* baby, not mine)
And really, who will go with me?
The LORD says, I'll go.
    Moses: Mean it?
The LORD says, Yes, yes; as you'll see.
    We'll really stand out, that's for sure.
The LORD says, Yes, yes; you I bless.
    But where is the proof positive?
The LORD says, My glory's my goodness,
Which means, I choose you, not you, me;
Mercy and graciousness are mine.
Such giving's what my goodness means;
The back you see, will be your sign.

A couple on a recent flight
Told me the Lord they also seek,
This text, however makes me think,
When Moses sees the LORD, oblique,
It's not that Moses just was mooned,
But it's the other way around—
The Lord's the one who seeks you out,
Let not your search such truth confound.

Matthew 22:15–22

Coin of the Realm

Some say that players should not take the knee
When others rise for "Oh, say can you see?"
They say that it's a mark of disrespect,
And verbally abuse those they'd correct.

It's something like when Jesus' enemies
Pulled out a coin for everyone to see,
And asked if he might choose to pay the tax
And thus the Law on idols he'd relax.

Instead, it was a broader truth he chose,
Which was that Caesar's head is juxtaposed
Against a faith God's sovereign over all,
Therefore, to Caesar, none should be in thrall.

These players don't forsake the waving flag,
But state a truth about which none should brag,
Which is that in this land made of the free,
Some cops give blacks more than the third degree.

They kneel in sorrow so opinions change,
So all for justice might now be engaged.
Not flag, but what it stands for is what saves:
Say kneelers who act out "home of the brave."

We are not free because arms make it so,
The Declaration's clear that we're bestowed
With rights by God, however you perceive;
So stand and kneel for all that you believe.

THE THIRTIETH SUNDAY IN ORDINARY TIME/
TWENTY-FIRST AFTER PENTECOST (A)—
MATTHEW 22:34–46; 1 THESSALONIANS 2:1–8

Matthew 22:34–46

The Fundamentalist

Though Jesus knows the point of metaphor,
Which is, unto the heart, an open door,
And knows you cannot parse how David's Lord
And son, Messiah, both are in accord,
He is a fundamentalist, it's clear,
On whether we should love our neighbor, dear,
For otherwise, one's faith is undercut.
Go, love, he says; no ifs or ands or buts.

1 Thessalonians 2:1–8

The Doctor Who's a Nurse

The pastor prayed for Dr. Hatch
Who'd known he could not stay detached
From human need, and thus has dared
To give, to those he might, God's care.
I know not if he calls it such;
I know not, if he prays, how much,
Or if he thinks that he's been called;
But this I know: that writer Paul,
When speaking of the tender nurse
Whose gentle care for children mercy
Shows, cares more for deeds than words,
And giving self is grace conferred.

(This poem is based on the story of a doctor who went from Worcester, Massachusetts, to Liberia, learned how to put on and take off the protective gear, and, when caring for a pastor with Ebola, found himself prayed for before the pastor died: http://nyti. ms/1rh6007.)

THE THIRTY-FIRST SUNDAY IN ORDINARY TIME/ TWENTY-SECOND AFTER PENTECOST (A)— JOSHUA 3:7–17; MATTHEW 23:1–12

Joshua 3:7–17

A Nation Where All Are Saved

The text progresses, as it must;
not Moses, out alone, or just
this Joshua, either, at this river,
this new, dividing sea the Giver
parts; but now, instead of one,
it looks like twelve ensure undone
the chaos that would interfere
with what the LORD would engineer.
They venture out into the deep,
which is no more, but just a heap
on their right hand, while on their left,
no waters stand; and they are blessed
to be a nation now, where all are saved—
Let us just like those Jordan priests behave.

Matthew 23:1–12

"Teacher," "Rabbi" and the Like

We Presbyterians now name
Our ministers for tasks reclaimed:
We're "teaching elders," for our role
That all may learn, in mind and soul,
God's grace. And Catholics still refer
To priests as "Father," which confers
A status that implies their love
To those below from God above.
Thus, Jesus' words now give me pause
In hope that he laid down no laws
Prohibiting what we are called!
But rather, pray he's still appalled
By any flouting ordination
As meaning character inflation.

THE THIRTY-SECOND SUNDAY IN ORDINARY TIME/TWENTY-THIRD AFTER PENTECOST (A)— JOSHUA 24:1-3a, 14-25; MATTHEW 25:1-13

Joshua 24:1-3a, 14-25

Not the Good Old Days

Once to every one and nation
Comes the moment to decide;
Sometimes hymns, though out of favor,
Tell a truth from which we hide.

Glibly, we imagine back in
"Bible times," "their" faith was strong;
Surely God spoke clearly, therefore
Many for the past now long.

Joshua didn't see it that way:
"Our ancestors got it wrong!
Gods were served beyond the river,
Now's the time for a new song!"

New occasions teach new duties,
Time makes ancient good uncouth,
Faith means always new decisions,
Chosen grace is each day's truth.

(The first two lines of the first and last stanzas come from the 1845 poem by James R. Lowell that he wrote as a protest against the U. S.'s war with Mexico, and which was put to Thomas J. Williams' tune EBENEZER.)

Matthew 25:1–13

On Time God

"Don't you hate it when that happens?"
Jesus says about that wedding
Where some bridesmaids missed the party
That they thought they'd be attending.

No one here is being callous,
It was simply customary;
Bridesmaids who could join inside were
Those who'd planned, and had not tarried.

Grace does not appear on schedule,
Like an entry on your smart phone;
Opportunities to love are
Tests of faith, and even backbone.

"He's an on time God," the song goes,
"Might not come just when you want him,
He'll be there right on time," which means,
Not being ready, will not stop him.

Don't miss the love that's put before you,
For it will come, and not ignore you.

THE THIRTY-THIRD SUNDAY IN ORDINARY TIME/
TWENTY-FOURTH AFTER PENTECOST (A)—
JUDGES 4:1-7 (8-24); MATTHEW 25:14-30

Judges 4:1-7 (8-24)

Wonderwomen

I think that not too many know
This ancient, Wonderwomen tale,
Where, Barak asks a prophetess
To go with him before he sails
To battle a strong enemy,
As guarantee he would not fail.

Or does he ask to humor her,
A woman who'd command a male?
Or could it be he's worried that
His aspirations she'd assail,
And like some prequel of Uriah,
He'd be the one to be impaled?

At any rate, she says she'll go,
Though goes with him to no avail,
That is, no glory will he earn;
Another woman will derail
The plans of Sisera, who burns
To conquer Israel, yet fails.

Soon Sisera will be no more,
His gory end makes us inhale;
But though, to us, the ethics of
Jael seem dubious and frail,
God's purposes for those oppressed
Will, by God's chosen means, prevail.

(Note: It's a shame the lectionary designers stop at verse 7, which in my view pretty much misses the point of the story. Go at least through verse 9. Consider going even further in Sunday worship, which in this case means telling the rest of the story, which includes Jael, as long as we realize it's meant to make us smile at how God will do in a cruel oppressor by whatever means will do the trick.)

Matthew 25:14–30

Treasure This

Beware that you don't use this text
To be the means whereby the next
Year's budget you might "make" converges
With what it seems the story urges.

One talent being far too much
For common laborers to touch,
It speaks, instead, of what is gained
When nothing you did, you attained.

Those overwhelmed by all they have,
Who know that all they are, God gave,
In joy, astounded by their treasure,
Know greatest gifts cannot be measured.

But those who try to make it last,
In worry they'll lose all amassed,
Have entered now into the hell
Which only trust in grace dispels.

CHRIST THE KING (REIGN OF CHRIST) SUNDAY (A)— EZEKIEL 34:11-16, 20-24; MATTHEW 25:31-46

Ezekiel 34:11-16, 20-24

The Once and Future Comeuppance of the Butters

The word I like the best within this text is "butted;"
I like how God's not happy with the sheep who strutted,
Who pushed and shoved their way around like some big wheel,
And turned the lives of others into an ordeal;
They make me think of big shots now, pontificating,
Who, on high horses, set about eliminating
The things that help all people in their daily living,
While claiming they know best, but to themselves they're giving!
Dear God, we need a David, shepherding the people,
Instead of those who would our commonwealth enfeeble;
O, kick their butts in any upcoming elections,
That words and acts for all might see a resurrection.

Matthew 25:31–46

Surprise!

The Gospel is about surprise!
Forget the habit to surmise
Just how you might reap some reward,
Or fear that you might be ignored
By God, say, when you're at the end,
And wonder if you might ascend,
Or descend, so to speak. You'll find
God's system of reward is blind
To whether you had made the grade!
No matter what, you'll be dismayed,
Since God's less likely to be bribed,
And more inclined to be described
As Christ, who so inspires your love
That, focused less on God above,
You'll worry not, nor will you gloat,
To be a hero, or a goat,
But simply offer all your care
To needy angels unawares.

Scripture Index

SCRIPTURE INDEX

SCRIPTURE INDEX

Title Index

CPSIA information can be obtained
at www.ICGtesting.com
Printed in the USA
BVHW042026230120
569692BV00013B/29